McKinney

MW01224242

Creating Meaningful Performance Assessments: Fundamental Concepts

Stephen N. Elliott

Published by
The Council for Exceptional Children

A Product of the
ERIC/OSEP Special Project
The ERIC Clearinghouse on
Disabilities and Gifted Education

Library of Congress Cataloging-in-Publication Data

Elliott, Stephen N.
   Creating meaningful performance assessments : fundamental concepts
/ Stephen N. Elliott.
       p. cm.—(CEC mini-library performance assessment)
   "A product of the ERIC\OSEP Special Project, the ERIC Clearinghouse on
Disabilities and Gifted Education."
   Includes bibliographical references (p.).
   ISBN 0-86586-249-4
   1. Criterion-referenced tests. 2. Exceptional children—Rating
of. I. Council for Exceptional Children.   II. ERIC/OSEP Special
Project.   III. Title.   IV. Series.
   LB3060.32.C74E45 1994
   371.2'71—dc20   94-17715
                                                             CIP

ISBN 0-86586-249-4

A product of the ERIC/OSEP Special Project, the ERIC Clearinghouse on
Disabilities and Gifted Education

Published in 1994 by The Council for Exceptional Children, 1920 Association
Drive, Reston, Virginia 22091-1589

Stock No. P5059

This publication was prepared with funding from the U.S. Department of
Education, Office of Special Education Programs, contract no. RR93002005.
Contractors undertaking such projects under government sponsorship are
encouraged to express freely their judgment in professional and technical
matters. Prior to publication the manuscript was submitted for critical review
and determination of professional competence. This publication has met such
standards. Points of view, however, do not necessarily represent the official
view or opinions of either The Council for Exceptional Children or the
Department of Education.

Printed in the United States of America

10 9 8 7 6 5 4 3 2

Foreword

CEC's policy on inclusive schools and community settings invites all educators, other professionals, and family members to work together to create early intervention, educational, and vocational programs and experiences that are collegial, inclusive, and responsive to the diversity of children, youth, and young adults. Policymakers at the highest levels of state/provincial and local government, as well as school administration, also must support inclusive principles in the educational reforms they espouse.

One area in which the inclusion of students with disabilities is critical is the development and use of new forms of assessment. This is especially true when assessment becomes a tool by which local school districts, states, and our nation show accountability for the education of students.

As multidimensional instruments that can cross curriculum areas, performance assessments have the potential to be powerful instructional tools as well as tools for accountability. As this new technology is applied in creating new assessment instruments, students with disabilities must be considered during the design of the assessment, administration, scoring, and reporting of results.

CEC is proud to contribute this Mini-Library to the literature on performance assessment, and in so doing to foster the appropiate inclusion of students with disabilities in this emerging technology for instruction and accountability.

Preface

Performance assessment, authentic assessment, portfolio assessment—these are the watchwords of a new movement in educational testing. Its advocates say this movement is taking us beyond the era when the number 2 pencil was seen as an instrument of divine revelation. Its critics say it is just another educational bandwagon carrying a load of untested techniques and unrealistic expectations.

Despite the criticisms and reservations that are sometimes expressed, these new approaches are being implemented in a growing number of large-scale assessment programs at federal, state, and district levels. They are also finding their way into small-scale use at school and classroom levels.

What about students with disabilities? Are the new assessment techniques more valid than conventional assessment techniques for these students? Are the techniques reliable and technically sound? Will they help or hinder the inclusion of students with disabilities in large-scale assessment programs? Can classroom teachers use the techniques to assess student learning and possibly enrich the classroom curriculum? The following fictional vignettes illustrate some of these issues.

Vignette 1

The State of Yorksylvania developed educational standards and a statewide system of student assessments to monitor progress in achieving the standards. The use of standardized multiple-choice tests was rejected because these tests were thought to trivialize education. It was feared that teachers would "teach down" to the tests rather than "teach up" to the standards. So, committees of teachers, parents, and employers were formed to translate the standards into "authentic" performance assessments. The resulting assessment system was called the Yorksylvania Performance Inventory (YPI).

Once a year, students from every school in the state were administered the YPI, which consisted of several assessments, each of which required up to 3 days to complete. Students worked, sometimes individually and sometimes in small groups, on tests involving complex, high-level tasks that crossed curriculum areas. In one task, students individually did research and answered essay questions interrelating the geography, wildlife, and history of their state. In another task, students worked in groups to design a car powered by fermentation. Schools were provided with practice activities and curriculum guides to encourage the infusion of performance assessment activities into the school curriculum.

The state policy allowed special education students to be included in the YPI, excluded, or provided with special modifications, depending on their individual needs as indicated in their individualized education programs. Initially, most special education teachers supported the YPI because they felt it eliminated some artificial barriers (reading, test-taking skills, etc.) that put their students at a disadvantage on other types of tests. However, there were some questions and issues, such as the following:

- Some of the YPI tasks involved *a lot* of reading, more than was found on previous types of tests.

- Special education teachers sometimes felt pressured to exclude their students from testing in order to increase the school's scores.

- Special education students sometimes experienced extreme frustration in the YPI assessments, many of which bore no resemblance to these students' other schoolwork.

- Some parents of special education students questioned whether the standards were really applicable to their children and whether the YPI was diverting instruction from more relevant and important topics.

Vignette 2

A teacher named Pat had students at a wide range of functioning levels, including a number of mainstreamed students receiving special education services. Pat was always on the lookout for new ideas and approaches. Pat began reading articles and attending conferences on new assessment approaches termed *portfolio assessment, authentic assessment, per-*

formance assessment, and *alternative assessment.* These approaches seemed to make a lot of sense, and Pat decided to try them out. One of the first approaches Pat tried was authentic assessment. Rather than simply testing students on their rote learning of skills and content, Pat began to look for ways to use realistic, complex activities to test whether the students could actually apply what they learned. For example, Pat combined writing, spelling, science, and career skills into an activity in which students wrote letters of application for jobs as physicists, biologists, or chemists. Pat particularly valued activities that engaged students in solving interesting problems. For example, after a unit on optics, Pat assigned students to draw a diagram explaining why mirrors reverse an image from left to right but not from top to bottom. The students grappled with that problem for several days.

Pat liked the holistic scoring procedures developed in these new assessment approaches. Rather than simply marking a response correct or incorrect, Pat scored student work on a number of dimensions (e.g., analysis of the problem, clarity of communication) according to meaningful quality criteria. The development of authentic performance tasks and scoring procedures helped Pat clarify the most important learning outcomes.

Pat also liked the idea of portfolio assessment, in which students could select and collect "best pieces" to demonstrate their learning and achievement during the year. Student self-evaluation became a valued part of this process.

In all, Pat was very pleased with these new assessment approaches and intended to continue using them. Instruction became more activity based and more focused on real-world uses of the material. There were, however, some issues that Pat began to think about:

• Students with deficits in certain academic areas, notably writing, were at a real disadvantage. It was sometimes hard to determine whether an inadequate response resulted from poor writing skills, poor mastery of the content, poor problem-solving skills, lack of creativity, or some combination of these factors. Pat considered allowing some students to tape record their responses, but decided not to. Wasn't writing itself an authentic task required in the real world?

- Pat wasn't sure how to use the information provided by these tests to plan additional instruction, particularly if a student was having difficulty.

- Pat wondered how to tell whether or not an activity was in fact authentic, especially for students whose adult lives would be very different from Pat's own.

In 1992, the Division of Innovation and Development (DID) in the U.S. Department of Education's Office of Special Education Programs and the ERIC/OSEP Special Project of The Council for Exceptional Children formed a Performance Assessment Working Group to discuss issues such as these. The term *performance assessment* was adopted as a general designation for the range of approaches that include performance assessment, authentic assessment, alternative assessment, and portfolio assessment.

Performance assessment was defined has having the following characteristics:

1. *The student is required to create an answer or a product rather than simply fill in a blank, select a correct answer from a list, or decide whether a statement is true or false.*

2. *The tasks are intended to be "authentic."* The conventional approach to test development involves selecting items that represent curricular areas or theoretical constructs, and that have desired technical characteristics (e.g. they correlated with other similar items, they discriminated between groups, etc.). Authentic tasks, on the other hand, are selected because they are "valued in their own right"[1] rather than being "proxies or estimators of actual learning goals."[2]

The Performance Assessment Working Group produced this series of four Mini-Library books on various topics related to performance assessment and students with disabilities. In *National and State Perspectives on Performance Assessment and Students with Disabilities,* Martha Thurlow discusses trends in the use of performance assessment in large-scale testing programs. In *Performance Assessment and Students with Disabilities: Usage in Outcomes-Based Accountability Systems,* Margaret McLaughlin and Sandra Hopfengardner Warren describe the experi-

[1]R. L. Linn, E. L. Baker, & S. B. Dunbar. (1991). Complex, performance-based assessment: Expectations and validation criteria. *Educational Researcher, 20*(8), 15–21.
[2]M. W. Kirst. (1991). Interview on assessment issues with Lorrie Shepard. *Educational Researcher, 20*(2), 21–23, 27.

ences of state and local school districts in implementing performance assessment. In *Creating Meaningful Performance Assessments: Fundamental Concepts*, Stephen Elliott discusses some of the key technical issues involved in the use of performance assessment. And, in *Connecting Performance Assessment to Instruction*, Lynn Fuchs discusses the classroom use of performance assessment by teachers.

Martha J. Coutinho
University of Central Florida

David B. Malouf
U.S. Office of Special Education Programs

August, 1994

Members of the Performance Assessment Work Group

Joan Baron, Performance Assessment Collaborative for Education, Harvard University

Joyce Choate, Council for Exceptional Diagnostic Services, Northeast Louisiana University

Lorraine Costella, Frederick County, Maryland, Public Schools

Martha Coutinho, Division of Innovation and Development, U.S. Office of Special Education Programs

Stephen Elliott, University of Wisconsin-Madison

Lynn Fuchs, Vanderbilt University

John Haigh, Maryland State Department of Education

Larry Irvin, University of Oregon

Robert Linn, Center for Research on Evaluation, Standards, and Student Testing

Lynn Malarz, Association for Supervision and Curriculum Development

David Malouf, Division of Innovation and Development, U.S. Office of Special Education Programs

Margaret McLaughlin, Center for Policy Options in Special Education, University of Maryland

Trina Osher, National Association of State Directors of Special Education

James Poteet, Council for Educational Diagnostic Services, Ball State University

Clay Starlin, Western Regional Resource Center, University of Oregon

Martha Thurlow, National Center on Educational Outcomes for Students with Disabilities, University of Minnesota

Sandra Hopfengardner Warren, Center for Policy Options in Special Education, University of Maryland

Note. Members' affiliations may have changed since the work group was formed.

About the Author

Stephen N. Elliott is Professor of Educational Psychology at the University of Wisconsin at Madison. He is also an Associate in the Wisconsin Center for Educational Research, where he codirects federal grants and works as a technical consultant on the Wisconsin Student Assessment System Project.

Most of Dr. Elliott's research has focused on the assessment and treatment of children's social behavior problems. His empirical work led him to develop the *Social Skills Rating System*, a nationally standardized rating scale and a coordinated treatment manual. These products are used in schools throughout the United States and Canada.

Dr. Elliott has authored many journal articles, convention papers, and books for graduate training and professionals. Throughout his career, his work has received much professional recognition: He was the recipient of the 1984 Lightner Witmer Award from the American Psychological Association, has been a Fellow of four divisions of the American Psychological Association, and served as editor of the *School Psychology Review* for two terms (1985–1990). He has served on the executive boards of the Council of Directors of School Psychology Programs, the Accreditation Steering Committee of the American Psychological Society, and is currently on the editorial boards of four journals. He is a frequent consultant to school systems concerning child assessment issues and a frequent speaker at professional development programs in the United States and Canada.

Dr. Elliott became interested in performance assessment in 1990, as a parent of two children whose school system asked him to help revise how they assessed students' learning. Along with several educators and community members, Dr. Elliott led an action committee on authentic assessment that proposed a major reconceptualization of student assessment. The work in his own children's school system served as a springboard for his further readings, research, and speaking about assessments that have the potential to be instructionally valid and personally meaningful to students.

Contents

PART I.
THE EVOLUTION OF PERFORMANCE ASSESSMENT: WHERE DO WE STAND?

Testing and the assessment of children's academic progress have become focal issues of educational reform activities in the 1990s. Leading educators and many consumers want assessment methods to cover content that represents "important" educational outcomes, to challenge students to use higher-order thinking skills and apply their knowledge, and to inform teaching (Stiggins, 1991; Wolf, LeMahieu, & Eresh, 1992). In short, it seems that many educational stakeholders are calling for assessment to drive instruction and to measure a range of achievement outcomes from ready-to-work skills to high-level reasoning with math and science concepts. This is asking a lot. However, given the assumption that "what you test is what you teach," this emphasis on assessment as a vehicle for reform should not be surprising.

Special educators have not been involved in many aspects of recent educational reform efforts, but they have had much to contribute to assessment practices and instruction. Perhaps one reason for the omission of special educators and students with disabilities from the assessment reform discussions is that statewide, on-demand types of assessments historically have not included or accommodated many students with disabilities (Ysseldyke & Thurlow, 1993a).

The literature on performance assessment and the rationale for its increased use reflects strong parallels to curriculum-based measurement (Deno, 1985; Shinn, 1989) and behavioral assessment (Kratochwill & Sheridan, 1990) methods. Fuchs (1994), in an accompanying book in this series, provides an excellent comparative analysis of these approaches to performance assessment. Prior to Fuchs's work, there have not been any direct references acknowledging these similarities or the theoretical and technical knowledge base for these alternative assessment methods.

Similarly, little has been written in the special education literature about performance (authentic) assessment until very recently (e.g., Poteet, Choate, & Stewart, 1993)

Whatever their educational background, educators share a common desire for more assessments that are relatively low-inference, objective measures of important learning outcomes that lead to instructional actions. Since performance assessments have been touted as offering these features, they deserve serious attention from educators of all students.

Performance assessment recently has become one of the most written about alternative methods to norm-referenced tests. Yet, there are few empirical investigations into the efficacy of performance assessments and no published reports about using performance assessment methods to evaluate the academic functioning of students with disabilities or those who are educationally at risk. This lack of data has done little to slow endorsements of performance assessment, however, for as Madaus (1985) observed several years ago, "testing is the darling of policymakers across the country" (p. 5).

Although policymakers may find testing a "darling," educators and psychometricians involved in the actual development and use of performance tests and related assessment procedures are discovering some significant technical and practical challenges. This book examines fundamental technical and implementation issues involved with large-scale, on-demand performance assessments and teacher-constructed, classroom-based performance assessments. The purposes and consequences of these two types of assessments are often very different, and they require examination of a wide range of issues. To gain an understanding of the potential advantages and disadvantages of performance assessment, it is necessary to discuss its definitions and core concepts, examine sources of validity evidence, and analyze steps in the development and interpretation of an assessment task.

1. Definitions and Core Concepts

Performance assessment is defined as "testing methods that require students to create an answer or product that demonstrates their knowledge or skills" (U.S. Congress, Office of Technology Assessment [OTA], 1992, p. 17). It can take many forms, including conducting experiments, writing extended essays, or doing mathematical computations. Performance assessment is best understood as a continuum of assessment formats ranging from the simplest student-constructed responses to comprehensive demonstrations or collections of work over time. Whatever format, common features of performance assessments involve (a) students' construction rather than selection of a response; (b) direct observation of student behavior on tasks resembling those commonly required for functioning in the world outside school; and (c) illumination of students' learning and thinking processes along with their answers (OTA, 1992).

Performance and Authentic Assessment

As Coutinho and Malouf (1992) noted regarding performance assessment with students with disabilities, writers have used a variety of terms (e.g., *authentic, portfolio, alternative*) to refer to assessment methods featuring student-generated responses. The term *performance* emphasizes a *student's active generation of a response* and highlights the fact that the response is observable either directly or indirectly via a permanent product. The term *authentic* refers to the nature of the *task* and *context* in which an assessment occurs. The authenticity dimension of assessment has become an important issue for at least two reasons. First, most educators assume that the more realistic or authentic a task is, the more interesting it is to students. Thus, students' motivation to engage in and perform an "authentic" task is perceived to be much higher than it is for tasks that do not appear to be relevant "real-world" problems or issues. Second, for educators espousing an outcomes-oriented approach to education, it is important to focus assessments on complex sets of skills and conditions that are generalizable across disciplines.

Key Dimensions of Performance Assessment

The term *performance* is consistently used by authors discussing state-wide, on-demand assessments for which students must produce a detailed response, whereas the term *authentic* is used more often by educators to describe teacher-constructed or -managed classroom assessment tasks that students must perform. Any serious discussion of educational assessment must consider the key dimensions implicit to both terms.

Figure 1 highlights the performance and authenticity dimensions of educational assessment tasks. It also indicates that a common third dimension of a valid assessment task is that the content assessed represents the content taught. Figure 1 synthesizes three key dimensions that educators want to manipulate in their assessments of students' achievement: student response, nature of the task, and relevance to instruction.

As indicated in the figure, assessment tasks can be characterized as varying in the degree to which they are *performance in nature, authentic,* and *aligned with curriculum outcomes.* For example, a low-performance task might be filling in a bubble sheet or selecting the best answer by circling a letter, whereas a high-performance task might be writing and presenting a report of research or conducting a scientific experiment in a lab. Similarly, a low authenticity task might be reading isolated nonsense words or writing a list of teacher-generated spelling words, whereas a high-authenticity task might be reading a newspaper article or the directions for installing a phone recording system or writing a letter to a friend using words that are important to the student. Finally, an example of a task that has a low degree of alignment with curriculum outlines is one in which facts and concepts are taught, but application is assessed; one with a high degree of alignment teaches and assesses the application of facts and concepts. Many educators are searching for assessments that are relatively high on all three dimensions. That is, they want highly authentic or "real-world" tasks that clearly are connected to their instructional curriculum and require students to produce, rather than select, a response. Conceptually, such tasks would lie within the HIGH circle in Figure 1.

Performance assessment is not entirely new to many educators. For example, physical education, art, music, and vocational and technological arts teachers all use students' products or performances to determine whether or not learning objectives have been met. What is new is (a) the use of this form of assessment in the core curricular areas of math, science, language arts, and social studies; (b) the use of scoring criteria to influence and interpret performances; and (c) the encouragement of students to conduct self-assessments. Thus, many educators already use some "weak" forms of performance assessment. That is, they (a) ask

FIGURE 1
The Relationship Among Performance, Authenticity, and the Classroom Curriculum in an Assessment Task

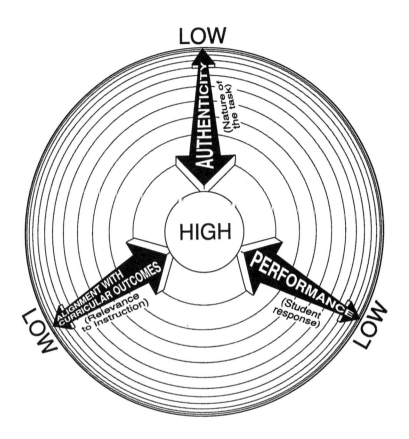

students to apply their knowledge and skills by producing a product and (b) provide students feedback about their performances in the form of grades. Besides these two traditional elements of performance assessment, the new, pedagogically stronger forms of performance assessment take steps to influence students' performances by:

1. Selecting assessment tasks that are clearly aligned or connected to what has been taught.

2. Sharing the scoring criteria for the assessment task with students prior to working on the task.

3. Providing students clear statements of standards and/or several models of acceptable performances before they attempt a task.

4. Encouraging students to complete self-assessments of their performances.

5. Interpreting students' performances by comparing them to standards that are developmentally appropriate, as well as to other students' performances.

Performance assessment is not new to educators. What is new is its use in core curriculum areas, the use of scoring criteria, and the encouragement of students to conduct self-assessments.

As conceptualized here, the stronger forms of performance assessment interact with instruction that precedes *and* follows an assessment task. This approach to assessment emphasizes the point that the *central purposes of most educational assessments are to facilitate communication among educational stakeholders—teachers, students, parents, administrators, employers—and to guide instruction.*

The central purposes of most educational assessments are to facilitate communication among educational stakeholders . . . and to guide instruction.

Reactivity and Consequences of Assessments

Many advocates of performance assessment (e.g., Archbald & Newmann, 1988; Wiggins, 1993) hope that authentic/performance assessments will be *reactive* in guiding or influencing instruction. That is, they believe that if teachers use assessments requiring students to produce something that is valued in the real world, something that is meaningful, then teachers will be more likely to adjust their curriculum to focus on real-world outcomes that are highly valued. Many state-level performance assessment projects currently under way seem to be counting on the fact that their assessment instruments (and scoring criteria) will be reactive. The issue of reactivity in assessment is not new, at least not to those familiar with behavioral assessment and the behavior change

---

research (Kazdin, 1974). In most assessment situations, assessors work hard to reduce or eliminate reactivity effects on the person being assessed. In the case of performance assessment, however, advocates are hoping that teachers and parents will react—that is, they will change their expectations about assessment outcomes and scoring criteria, which in turn will lead to improved student learning.

Reactivity of any performance assessment probably will be greatly influenced by the *consequences* (or stakes) of the assessment. If the consequences are significant (or high-stakes), change in instruction and content is likely to follow; if the consequences are insignificant (or low-stakes), change in instruction and content is not likely to occur. Collectively, the issues of reactivity and consequences of assessment lead to the technical issue of validity, in particular consequential validity (Messick, 1989). These issues are discussed in greater detail, along with other issues of reliability and validity in a later chapter.

From a classroom perspective, performance assessments would appear to allow more flexibility in the administration of tasks and offer an increased number of pathways for a learner to demonstrate command of the knowledge and skills required to accomplish a task. From an empirical perspective, evidence concerning the functioning of students with disabilities on performance assessments—whether the tasks are part of an on-demand large-scale assessment program or at the classroom level—is scarce. Given that at least 38 states in the United States presently are involved in the use or development of some form of statewide, on-demand performance assessment instruments (OTA, 1992), it seems clear that information about the use of performance assessments with students with disabilities is needed.

2. Theoretical Matters

Surprisingly little has been written about the theoretical aspects of performance assessment. Kratochwill (1992) noted the absence of a clear linkage to a theoretical base in the performance assessment literature and noted several advantages a linkage could offer developers and users of such performance assessment instruments. The advantages included (a) a conceptual framework to guide development, (b) information pertaining to empirical support for the inclusion of various assessment technologies, (c) guidelines for evaluation and refinement of the assessments, and (d) a framework for using the accumulation of knowledge within education and psychology about learners and learning.

Cognitive psychology and behavioral assessment are two fields with the potential to contribute to a theoretical base. Some authors have suggested that performance assessment is being driven by cognitive psychology, especially within the context of drawing distinctions between content (e.g., facts, concepts) and process knowledge (e.g., procedures, applications) (Archbald, 1991). Cognitive psychologists have provided much knowledge about influencing students' use of problem-solving strategies and the application of analytical skills, abilities that are of great interest to educators (e.g., Gardner, 1986; Resnick & Resnick, 1992). However, whether cognitive psychology can contribute to the measurement challenges in this area is highly debatable, as this approach is seen by many as having its most useful application in research and theory development rather than in real educational measurement problems (Mehrens, 1992).

Behavioral Assessment

Behavioral assessment can be defined as "the identification of meaningful response units and their controlling variables for the purposes of understanding and altering behavior" (Hayes, Nelson, & Jarrett, 1986, p. 464). Kratochwill noted that behavioral assessment is based on various theoretical models of behaviorism, including applied behavior analysis, neobehavioristic mediational S-R models, cognitive behavior modification, and social learning theory. A major characteristic of each of the approaches is that various environmental and situational influences are examined for their effect on behavior. Not only are these variables said to influence behavior during the assessment process, but their analysis and manipulation are linked to the development of effective instructional programs as well. This concern about the situational and environmental influences in an assessment parallels the motivations of developers of performance assessments, who want to design assessments that are authentic and challenging to learners and contain prompts, cues and scoring criteria that are pedagogically sound.

Performance assessments are conceptually aligned with a behavior assessment model rather than a norm-referenced psychometric model.

In an earlier article (Elliott, 1991), I characterized performance assessment as a neobehavioral approach to educational assessment because of (a) its heavy emphasis on the use of direct observations and permanent products in evaluating a person's behavior and (b) its concern for the authenticity of the task or performance situation. Given that most performance assessments are interpreted from an ideographic or criterion-referenced perspective, they are conceptually aligned with a behavior assessment model rather than a traditional norm-referenced psychometric model.

There is considerable knowledge to be gained from observing behavioral assessment in practice and the underlying theoretical assumptions. But perhaps more important, the empirical knowledge base that has been derived from work on the behavioral assessment of children's academic and social behavior is extensive, and it could provide direction to those using performance assessments (e.g., Kratochwill & Shapiro, 1988).

3. Current Research on Performance Assessment

The current research literature on performance assessment does not address critical issues in the assessment of students with disabilities. There is a developing literature, however, on performance assessments with minority students, some of whom may be considered to be at risk educationally. Reviews of literature in military performance assessments by Baker, O'Neil, Jr., and Linn (1993) and in education by Baker (1990) have reported that less than 5% of the literature is based on empirical data. Accounts of the reliability of scoring procedures have dominated the database studies.

Individual Differences

Several teams of researchers have been interested in how students of different experiences, abilities, and ethnic backgrounds do on performance assessment tasks. Shavelson and his colleagues conducted a series of studies concerning performance assessment in elementary science (Shavelson & Baxter, 1992; Shavelson, Baxter, & Pine, 1992; Shavelson et al. 1991). The researchers concluded that hands-on performance assessments in science can be produced that are reliable and capable of distinguishing students who have experienced hands-on science education from those who have been educated largely via textbook instruction.

The researchers also noted that their science performance assessments correlated only moderately with the Comprehensive Test of Basic Skills (CTBS), suggesting that the hands-on assessments are measuring a somewhat different achievement construct than that assessed on a standardized multiple-choice test. How students with disabilities would perform on these hands-on science tasks is unknown at this time; however, many of these hands-on tasks are intentionally less well defined than the traditional multiple-choice problems provided students (e.g., extraneous information may be included, procedures may not be extracted from answer stems, etc.). Thus, organizational skills and application of general problem-solving skills are required for good performance on many of the performance assessment tasks being used in statewide assessment programs. Coupled with the fact that the tasks are timed, it is likely that a significant percentage of students with learning disabilities would find these tasks both very challenging and frustrating. Accommodations and adaptations in presentation and response formats, time, and setting, as dictated by students' individual needs, would be necessary to avoid bias in testing this student population. Accommodations currently used in state testing programs are discussed in *National and State Perspectives on Performance Assessment and Students with Disabilities* by Martha L. Thurlow, in this mini-library.

With regard to the effects of background factors such as race or ethnicity, the evidence is mixed as to whether performance assessments increase or decrease bias (Cizek, 1991; Linn, Baker, & Dunbar, 1991). The National Assessment of Educational Progress (NAEP) reported that differences between African Americans and Caucasians were about the same on essay tests of writing and multiple-choice tests of reading. In Testing in American Schools (OTA, 1992), it was reported that experiences on the California Bar Exam indicated that minority differences are similar or possibly greater on performance tasks. Linn, Baker, and Dunbar (1991) found that African-American, Mexican-American, and Asian-American college students did better on direct measures of writing than on multiple-choice tests of written English. Using NAEP data, Koretz, Lewis, Skewes-Cox, and Burnstein (1992) reported that students differ by ethnicity in the rate at which they attempt more open-ended types of items.

Thus, the evidence concerning the use of performance assessment tasks with students from different ethnic and cultural backgrounds is unclear at this time. Some researchers have reported differences across cultural groups, whereas others have not. When differences have occurred, it has been unclear whether these differences were due to bias in content, actual differences among the participants tested, or bias in the scoring.

Task Specificity

Linn (1993) reported that experience with the use of performance-based measures in a variety of contexts indicates that performance on one task has only a weak to modest relationship to performance on another, even seemingly similar task. Examples of this observation can be found in ratings of students' written compositions (e.g., Dunbar, Koretz, & Hoover, 1991). Similarly, Shavelson and his colleagues, in the previously mentioned series of studies of performance assessment in elementary science, found that students' performances tend to vary widely from task to task, suggesting that upward of 10 to 20 tasks may be needed to evaluate science achievement reliably. Linn (1993) and others (Dunbar et al., 1991) have concluded that although raters do contribute to some of the variance in the characterization of performance results, with careful design of scoring criteria and good training, raters can provide highly consistent ratings. Thus, it seems the majority of variance in the performances of students is contributed by differences in their abilities and the difficulty of the tasks tested.

Scoring

The research suggests that we have reasonably well-developed models of rater training, maintenance of scale reliability, and verification of raters' use of predefined scoring rubrics (Baker, O'Neil, & Linn, 1993). This research has been done in virtually every school subject matter and across multiple grade levels. In most cases, the scoring has been done on students' written products, although some have scored students' oral performances from video (Hawkins, Collins, & Frederiksen, 1990) or via multimedia systems (Goldman, Pellegrino, & Bransford, in press). There is good evidence from work done both in the United States and abroad (Gipps, 1993; Queensland Department of Education, 1991) that scoring of large-scale performance assessment is feasible and can be done with high interrater reliability.

Finally, there is some evidence from statewide assessment programs with middle school and high school students that performance assessments result in relatively low levels of student performance in almost every subject matter area (Baker et al., 1993; Webb, 1993). This trend should be interpreted carefully, and it should raise questions about how instructional experiences are related to the assessment format, as well as about students' motivation to perform on these new assessment instruments. It seems that performance assessment tasks are more difficult than those on traditional tests; however, until more research is completed, issues of task difficulty remain unanswered.

It seems safe to conclude that performance assessment . . . is being advanced by dogma more than by data.

Need for a Research Base

Certainly, more is known about performance assessment than has been published in professional journals; however, it seems safe to conclude that performance assessment as a method to supplement, or replace, traditional multiple-choice tests is being advanced by dogma more than

---

data. Practically, it is an appealing approach for many educators, especially those interested in current reforms concerning outcomes and standards. However, the effects on students—especially students with disabilities and students who may be educationally at risk—are unknown. What is known is that more research is needed on performance assessment—in particular, research on the consequences of performance assessment for students who have disabilities or are at risk educationally and for their teachers.

The present research knowledge base regarding performance assessment is limited for a variety of reasons, central to which is the issue of validity and its related technical aspects. Advances in the use of performance assessments will be concurrent with the study of their validity. This is as it should be, for much of the data about the validity of an assessment instrument can only be gathered *after* the instrument has been used. Validity is both a conceptual and a technical issue at the center of all assessment activities. Therefore, the remainder of this book focuses on validity and several related technical issues that should be understood by potential users of performance assessment instruments whether they are large-scale (statewide) or teacher-constructed, classroom-based assessments.

PART II
TECHNICAL ISSUES IN DEVELOPING AND USING PERFORMANCE ASSESSMENT INSTRUMENTS

Implementation of performance assessments and related policy making are prompting test developers and psychometricians to rethink fundamental concepts of assessment and examine methods for ensuring high-quality assessment instruments. The technical challenges confronting test developers, especially with regard to large-scale or statewide performance assessments, are compounded by issues of time constraints and high-stakes use of results. Performance assessments generally are time intensive, and this creates practical dilemmas concerning breadth and depth of coverage. Performance assessments often have been promoted by policymakers who want to use their results to elevate standards of educational performance for individuals and entire schools. As the consequences for performances are increased, so are concerns about the comparability and corruptibility of performance assessment instruments (Baker et al., 1993; Linn, 1993: Mislevy, 1992). The dual concerns of time constraints and assessment consequences frequently associated with statewide assessments are also an issue of concern to classroom teachers and their students.

4. Validity and Its Bases

Central to the development and use of any assessment instrument is the conceptualization of *validity*. The validity of an assessment depends on the degree to which the interpretations and uses of assessment results are supported by empirical evidence and logical analysis. Thus, validation of an assessment instrument or process requires an evaluation of interpretations of results, as well as the intended and unintended consequences of using the assessment. In focusing on the consequences of an assessment, it becomes apparent that validity issues are in many ways issues of values.

Key Assumptions

Kane's (1992a, 1992b) work on validating performance assessments provides insights into key assumptions underlying the validation process and the relationship between validity and reliability. Specifically, Kane noted four key assumptions:

1. The domain of tasks from which the sample is drawn (the target domain) is appropriate for the skill being assessed.

2. Performance on a sample of tasks from the domain has been observed and evaluated in an appropriate way.

3. One can generalize from performance on the sample of tasks to expected performance over the domain of tasks.

4. There are no extraneous factors that have an undue influence on the results of the performance test. (1992a, p. 10)

Evaluative Criteria

Criteria for evaluating the validity of tests and related assessment instruments have long existed (e.g., Buros, 1933) and have been written about extensively (e.g., Cronbach, 1990; Wiggins, 1993). A joint committee of the American Educational Research Association, American Psychological Association, and National Council on Measurement in Education (1985) developed a comprehensive list of standards for tests that stressed the importance of construct validity. Extrapolating from this document, Baker and her associates (1993, p. 1214) enumerated five internal characteristics that valid performance assessments should exhibit:

1. Have meaning for students and teachers and motivate high performance.

2. Require the demonstration of complex cognitions . . . applicable to important problem areas.

3. Exemplify current standards of content or subject matter quality.

4. Minimize the effects of ancillary skills that are irrelevant to [the] focus of assessment.

5. Possess explicit standards for rating or judgment.

Given the approach to performance assessment that most states seem to be taking and the stated assumptions underlying the validation process, the most compelling forms of evidence needed to validate a performance assessment are generalizability data, interrater/interscorer reliability data, and judgments of the importance of the knowledge and skills required to successfully complete the tasks. Thus, evidence for the validity of a test or assessment instrument takes two forms: (1) how the test or assessment instrument "behaves" given the content covered and (2) the effects of using the test or assessment instrument.

Questions commonly asked about a test's "behavior" concern its relation to other measures of a similar construct, its ability to predict future performances, and its coverage of a content domain. Questions about the use of a test typically focus on the test's ability to reliably differentiate individuals into groups and to guide the methods teachers use to teach the subject matter covered by the test. Some questions arise about unintended uses of a test or assessment instrument. For example: Does use of the instrument result in discriminatory practices against various groups of individuals? Is it used to evaluate others (e.g., parents or teachers) who are not directly assessed by the test?

Messick (1988) best captured the complexities of judging an assessment instrument's validity, characterizing it as "an inductive summary of both the adequacy of existing evidence for and the appropriateness of potential consequences of test interpretation and use" (p. 34). Thus, Messick corrected the common misconception that validity lies *within* a test and went on to conceptualize validity as resting on the following four bases:

(1) an inductive summary of convergent and discriminant evidence that the test scores have a plausible meaning or construct interpretation, (2) an appraisal of the value implications of the test interpretation, (3) a rationale and evidence for the relevance of the construct and the utility of the scores in particular applications, and (4) an appraisal of the potential social consequences of the proposed use and of the actual consequences when used. (1988, p. 42)

Figure 2 provides a graphic representation of Messick's four bases of test validity. This figure indicates that test validity can be represented in terms of two facets connecting the source of the justification (i.e., evidential basis or consequential basis) to the function or outcome of the testing (i.e., interpretation or use). According to Messick (1988), this crossing of basis and function "provides a unified view of test validity" (p. 42). In a more recent article, Messick (1994) elaborated on the interplay between evidence and consequences in the validation of performance assessments. He concluded that, like all assessments, performance assessments "should be validated in terms of content, substantive, structural, external, generalizable, and consequential aspects of construct validity" (p. 22). Messick went on to advise developers of performance assessments to use a "construct-driven rather than a task-driven approach . . . because the meaning of the construct guides the selection or construction of relevant tasks as well as the rational development of scoring criteria and rubrics" (p. 22).

FIGURE 2
Facets of Test Validity

	Test Interpretation	Test Use
Evidential Basis	Construct Validity	Construct Validity + Relevance/Utility
Consequential Basis	Value Implications	Social Consequences

Note. From Messick (1988), p. 42

5. Technical Challenges Associated with Performance Assessments

Most of the statewide performance assessments being developed in the United States are apparently intended to be high stakes. In other words, their results would lead to significant consequences both for individuals and for schools or school districts. Given this assumption, the technical qualities of the instruments and the scoring procedures must meet high standards for reliability and validity.

The twin hallmarks of traditional tests, reliability and validity, require close examination and extension, because the new models of assessment, including performance assessments, are "located conceptually midway on the continuum between construct approaches and ideographic demonstration of complex performance" (Baker, O'Neil, Jr., & Linn, 1993, p. 1214) . Four related clusters of conceptual issues dominate most discussions about providing evidence for the reliability and validity of performance assessment instruments. These are: (1) assessment as a curriculum event, (2) task content alignment with curriculum and important educational outcomes, (3) scoring of results and subsequent communications with consumers, and (4) linking and comparing results over time.

Assessment as a Curriculum Event

The conceptualization of an assessment as a curriculum event is the direct result of work in language arts performance assessment. Many language arts educators see externally mandated assessments not only as insensitive to the integrity of the language arts instruction but also as demanding performances that are at odds with the performances that occur naturally in conjunction with integrated language arts instruction (Witte & Vander Ark, 1992). To overcome their concerns about externally mandated assessments, language arts educators have reconceptualized a test as a curriculum event—that is, as a series of theoretically and practically coherent learning activities structured in such a way that they lead to a single predetermined end.

The conceptualization of assessment as a curriculum event has ramifications for the content of an assessment instrument, the length and types of activities required to complete the assessment, the number of items in the assessment instrument, and the scoring. This conceptualization of assessment as a curriculum event presents some significant challenges to a traditional test theory model and subsequent tactics for documenting reliability and validity. Conversely, the conceptualization is consistent with many educators' perspectives of what assessment ought to be like, because it incorporates qualities that should make the results more meaningful and useful to educators and students alike.

Seeing Assessment as a curriculum event . . . should make the results more meaningful and useful to educators and students alike.

Regardless of subject matter area, as performance assessments take on the characteristics of strong performance assessments outlined earlier, the lines between what is assessment and what is instruction blur. Some performance assessment advocates (e.g., Wiggins, 1993) say this is as it should be, but for those concerned about documenting the technical qualities of an assessment, this blurring adds a significant burden to the task. Issues of instructional opportunities and equity also become more salient as the lines between assessment and instruction blur (Task Force Report on Cultural and Linguistic Diversity in Education, 1993).

Task Content Alignment with Curriculum

The perception that much of what is tested is not relevant or has not been taught in a classroom has been a source of concern to many educators and students. Another perception is that how information is tested influences students' performances. The concern about test content is multifaceted and is of central relevance to judgments about the reliability and validity of any assessment instrument. The relationships among curriculum content, task content, and important educational outcomes often are not under the control of one group. For statewide assessments, a strategy of using experienced classroom teachers to play the major role in the development of test items and materials is necessary to increase the likelihood that the content of assessments will be consistent with what is or can be taught in the classroom and with what is highly valued as an outcome of education.

Given the limited number of items that can be presented in a performance assessment as conceptualized in most statewide assessment programs, issues of domain definition and content sampling from the domain become critical. Specifically, there is a need for personnel involved in the development of statewide instruments in the content areas to provide a definition of their subject domain so that items and materials that are representative of various aspects of the domain can be sampled yearly. This issue of domain sampling also is highly relevant to discussions of task and instrument difficulty, and ultimately to judgments of comparability of instruments over time.

In statewide assessments, the use of experienced classroom teachers to develop test items and material increases the alignment of the assessment with the curriculum and with valued educational outcomes.

Content alignment between what is tested and what is taught generally is less of an issue with teacher-developed performance assessments than with formal statewide assessments. The related issue of what content should be covered and assessed for all students is a concern at the local level, and it is a particularly salient one for educators serving students with disabilities. Work done at the National Center on Educational Outcomes at the University of Minnesota, funded by the U.S. Department of Education, provides educators with a meaningful framework for conceptualizing valued outcomes for all students and formulating means for assessing these outcomes (Ysseldyke & Thurlow, 1993b). Performance assessments are part of the recommended assessment packet.

Scoring and Subsequent Communications with Consumers

The accurate and meaningful scoring of performance assessments is predicated on the development of descriptive scoring criteria, evaluative standards that are well-understood and developmentally appropriate, and well-trained raters. Typically, a general framework for scoring performance tasks features the use of Likert-type scales with multitrait anchoring descriptions that raters must use to characterize students' responses to each item. The anchor point labels are likely to be consistent across subject matter. For example, top performances are often characterized as "Exemplary Performances," whereas extremely poor performances, regardless of subject matter, are characterized as "Inadequate

Performances." Responses that are largely incomplete are characterized as "Unscorable Performances." Within this general scoring approach, ordinal category scores are rendered for various knowledge and skill area domains in a subject.

As presently conceptualized, the scoring and interpretation of performance assessment instruments is akin to a criterion-referenced approach to testing. A student's performance is evaluated by a trained rater who compares the student's responses to multitrait descriptions of performances and gives the student a single number corresponding to the description that best characterizes the performance. Students are compared directly to scoring criteria and only indirectly to each other.

Given this general approach to scoring (whereby teachers trained as scorers rate performances of students), high (e.g., 90%) interrater agreements and "blind" ratings (e.g., teachers rate students from schools other than those in which they teach) are essential features of a statewide performance assessment system. This approach to scoring is more labor intensive and time consuming than traditional multiple-choice tests, although it has the benefit of educating teachers about the content of the test and the characteristics of exemplary performances. Time and costs for scoring can be very high; however, they can be reduced if a sampling approach, rather than a census approach, is taken to scoring students' responses. In other words, instead of scoring all students' responses for the state's purposes of monitoring school and district performances, a representative sample (e.g., 20% to 25%) of the students from each school could be scored by raters from outside the school district. The tests for the remaining students could be scored locally by teachers if so desired. Thus, a local district could get detailed individual reports of performances for all of their students, while the state would get performance results for groups of students by grade within schools or school districts.

Time and costs for scoring can be reduced if a sampling approach, rather than a census approach, is taken.

When using performance assessment at the classroom level, it is unlikely that teachers would use a sampling approach to scoring. Every student needs feedback when the purpose of assessment is diagnosis and monitoring of student progress. Many advocates of performance assessment encourage teachers to show students how to assess their own performances. This is possible when the scoring criteria are well articulated and teachers are comfortable with having students share in their own evaluation process. Many special educators have used self-monitoring or self-evaluation interventions for years with some of their students, so it seems reasonable that they would be receptive to some of the self-assessment aspects of performance assessment.

Linking and Comparing Results Over Time

Several of the major outcomes-related questions that have stimulated the development of performance assessment instruments by states concern comparisons of students over time and across grade levels. Therefore, methods are needed to facilitate reliable and meaningful comparisons of students' performances. Statistical and judgmental methods have been developed to accomplish this goal. Linn (1992) has referred to these as *linking* methods. Linking, according to Linn, is a generic term that includes a variety of approaches to making results of one assessment comparable to those of another. A variety of other terms (e.g., *anchoring, benchmarking, calibration, equating, prediction, projection, scaling, statistical moderation, social moderation, verification,* and *auditing*) have been used to characterize approaches to comparing results from different assessments. Tables 1 and 2 provide a description of the most frequently used terms and requirements for using the methods.

For most purposes of performance assessments, the two approaches to linking that seem most appropriate and manageable are statistical moderation and social moderation. The statistical moderation approach is used to compare performances across content areas (e.g., math to language arts) for groups of students who have taken a test at the same point in time. The social moderation approach to linking is a judgmental approach that is built on consensus of raters. In the use of social moderation, the comparability of scores assigned depends substantially on the development of consensus among professionals. This process serves to verify samples of performances at successively higher levels in a system (e.g., class, school, district, and state) and to function as an audit. As noted in Table 2, the social moderation approach substitutes requirements for developing professional consensus regarding standards and exemplars of performances meeting those standards for the more familiar measurement and statistical requirements associated with statistical moderation. Linking assessments over a period of 1 or 2 years generally is not a concern of classroom teachers, who use performance-based assessments to evaluate individual students in each new class, rather than to directly compare classes over the course of several years.

TABLE 1
Description of, Requirements for, and Examples of
Five Forms of Linking Distinct Assessments

Form of Linking	Description	Requirements	Example
Equating	Strongest form of linking. Any interpretation justified for one form of test is also justified for equated form.	Most demanding form of linking. Forms must measure the same construct with equal degree of reliability. Forms are interchangeable.	New versions of a state test used to certify high school graduates are introduced each year. It is desired that the score required for graduation is equivalent from one year to the next.
Calibration (includes vertical equating)	Different techniques of linking generally needed to support individual and group interpretations. Linking giving the right answer to most likely score on other form for individual student, in general, will give the wrong answer to questions about distributions for groups (e.g., percent of students in state scoring at the advanced level on NAEP) and vice versa.	Must measure the same construct. But may differ in reliability. May also differ in the level at which the measures are most useful (e.g., forms designed for students at different grade levels).	A state uses a version of a test that is shorter than a national test but designed to measure the same skills. The state version is less reliable than the national test due to its reduced length. Estimates of the percentage of students in the state who score above selected points on the national test are desired.
Statistical Moderation	Comparisons are made among scores provided by different sources (e.g., teachers) or different subject matter areas (e.g., English, math, history). Statistical moderation is used to adjust scores in an effort to make them "comparable." Comparability is imperfect and may give unknown advantage to one locale or content area relative to another.	Some external examination or anchor measure is needed to adjust local scores or scores on different subject area examinations. Utility depends heavily on the relevance of the external examination or anchor test and on the strength of its relationship with the locally defined or subject area examinations.	As assessment system consists of a combination of extended response questions that are scored locally by teachers and a standardized test that is administered under controlled conditions and scored centrally. The standardized test is used to adjust for between-school differences in teacher assigned scores on the locally-scored questions.

continues

23

TABLE 1 (Continued)

Form of Linking	Description	Requirements	Example
Prediction (also called projection)	The weakest form of statistical linking. The predictions are heavily dependent on context, group used to establish a relationship, and time. Predictions that hold for one group (e.g., males) may not hold for another (e.g., females) or for a combination of groups (e.g., males and females).	Predictions can be made as long as there is a relationship between measures. The precision of the prediction will depend on the strength of the relationship. Due to sensitivity of prediction to context, group, and time, the prediction needs to be re-evaluated frequently.	Performance on a multiple-choice test is obtained and used to predict performance on an essay test. Different prediction systems are used for predicting performance for individual students and for predicting group distributional characteristics.
Social Moderation (also called consensus moderation, auditing, verification)	Performances on distinct tasks are rated using a common framework and interpreted in terms of a common standard (e.g., essays written in response to prompts used in state A and different prompts in state B are interpreted in terms of the same national standards).	The primary requirements are concerned with the development of a consensus on definitions of standards and on the performances that meet those standards. Staff development and review of discrepancies in ratings are critical. Ratings assigned by local teachers may be compared to independently assigned ratings from other raters and the latter may be used to adjust local scores. Documentation needs to be provided regarding the degree to which different sets of judges agree that given responses to different tasks meet common standards.	States or groups of states develop their own sets of performance-based assessments in reference to a common content framework. Scoring of performance depends heavily on professional judgments of teachers and a system of spot checks and verification. Nonetheless, it is expected that performance of individual students, schools, districts and states will be compared to a single set of national standards.

Source. Linn (1992)

TABLE 2
Requirements of Different Techniques of
Linking Distinct Assessments

Requirements for Assessments	Type of Linking				
	EQ^1	CAL^2	$STAT$ MOD^3	PRE^4	SOC MOD^5
Measure same thing (construct)	yes	yes	no	no	no
Equal reliability	yes	no	no	no	no
Equal measurement precision throughout the range of levels of student achievement	yes	no	no	no	no
A common external examination	no	no	yes	no	no
Different conversion to go from test X to Y than from Y to X	no	maybe	NA	yes	no
Different conversions for estimates for individuals and for group distributional characteristics	no	yes	no	yes	no
Frequent checks for stability over contexts, groups, and time required	no	yes	yes	yes	yes
Consensus on standards and on exemplars of performance	no	no	no	no	yes
Credible, trained judges to make results comparable	no	no	no	no	yes

[1] Equating
[2] Calibration
[3] Statistical Moderation
[4] Predication
[5] Social Moderation

Source. Linn (1992).

6. Information Needed to Advance the Use of Performance Assessments

Educators have covered significant conceptual ground in the development and use of performance assessment instruments with students in the mainstream. Little, however, has been done to ensure or at least understand how students with disabilities are likely to be affected by performance assessments. Many issues, both technical and practical, remain. The fundamental issue of inclusion of students with disabilities in state and national assessment programs, many of which are or soon will be including performance assessment components, recently was addressed in an NCEO report (Ysseldyke & Thurlow, 1993a) titled *Inclusion and Testing Accommodations for Students with Disabilities.* Reschly (1993) explained that inclusion decisions historically have varied with specific outcome domains and the stakes of results. Generally, as the consequences of an assessment increase, there has been an unwarranted exclusion of students with disabilities. Reschly and several others (i.e., Algozzine, 1993; Reynolds, 1993) who authored position papers for the NCEO report argued for full or nearly full inclusion of students with disabilities. In contrast, Merwin (1993) took the position that it is acceptable to exclude children with disabilities because they represent a relatively small number of students. Merwin did acknowledge, however, that validity research on the performances of students with disabilities on large-scale assessments was still needed. He suggested that the inclusion issue is directly related to several other technical issues such as reliability, score aggregation, and sampling.

Based on the existing research literature on performance assessments and awareness of general concerns about the assessment of students with disabilities, the following short list of issues is recommended for conceptual work and empirical investigations:

Generally, as the consequences of an assessment increase, there has been an unwarranted exclusion of students with disabilities.

- *Fairness or Bias.* Methods for preventing or reducing bias must be enumerated, and procedures for determining bias must be built in to the field testing and scoring of the various performance assessments.

- *Comparability of Tasks.* Methods for documenting the nature of performance tasks must be developed so variables of task content, task difficulty, and task value can be operationalized and communicated.

- *Consequences of Performance Assessments.* Procedures for documenting the intended and unintended consequences of performance assessments must be designed, and related data should be collected as part of the field-testing programs. In addition, data on costs for conducting large-scale performance assessments need to be gathered.

Performance assessments hold significant promise for enhancing the instruction and evaluation of students, yet before they become a viable reality for use with all students, many technical questions require empirical and pragmatic, answers. In addition, educators need to address the following implementation issues:

1. Selection of educational outcomes to guide assessments.

2. Identification of indicators of progress toward targeted outcomes.

3. Development of methods for assessing performance on these indicators and/or outcomes.

4. Development and refinement of criteria for scoring students' performances and standards for interpreting performances.

5. Creation of teacher training opportunities to enhance understanding and use of performance assessments.

6. Stimulation of system support and resources needed to facilitate alternative assessments.

Collectively, these implementation concerns represent significant pieces of the performance assessment puzzle (Elliott, 1993; see Figure 3). They require the attention of researchers and educators alike if performance assessment practices are to be usable with a large number of students with disabilities.

FIGURE 3
Implementation Pieces of the Performance Assessment Puzzle

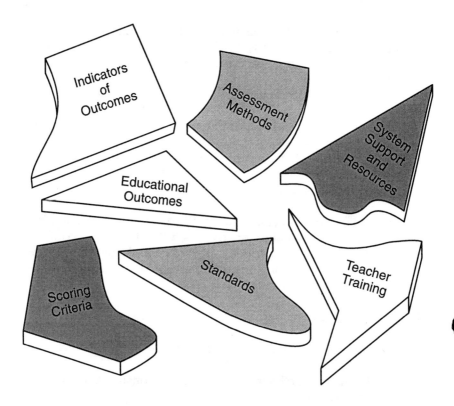

7. Conclusion: Proceed with Caution

Expectations for performance assessments seem extremely high, yet the conceptual and technical underpinnings of these assessments are just beginning to be understood. Traditional models of test development and validation are being stretched, instructional practices are being reconceptualized with assessment as a centerpiece, and statements about rigorous outcomes for all students are being made more loudly and frequently. Changes are occurring in many educational locales. Some of the suggested changes are theoretically and practically familiar to special educators, who have for decades been adapting assessments to provide more insights into instruction. For example, adoption of behavioral assessment models that honor individual variability as meaningful information (rather than as measurement error), and use of mastery learning approaches where what is taught is tested and re-tested, are common approaches shared by many special educators and current reformers of educational assessment practices. More common ground is needed, however, if students with disabilities are to share in the purported benefits of performance assessments. The first practical step is one of inclusion—inclusion in statewide assessment programs, in local educators' discussions of classroom assessment, and in the research programs of the technical experts studying the characteristics and qualities of performance assessments.

Performance assessment is a promising philosophy and method of assessment that may have some significant practical benefits for all students and educators. Strong forms of performance assessments are achievable in the classroom, where teachers have control of instructional outcomes and the instructional environment so that assessment criteria and feedback can be used to enhance learning. Apparently, all students can benefit from the classroom use of performance assessments, and many of the technical concerns are minimized at the classroom level, given the lower stakes associated with classroom-based decisions. With regard to the use of performance assessments in state-wide assessment programs, where stakes are presumed to be high, more data are needed to temper dogma and ensure quality.

References

Algozzine, B. (1993). Including students with disabilities in systemic efforts to measure outcomes: Why ask why? In J. E. Ysseldyke & M. L. Thurlow (Eds.), *Views on inclusion and testing accommodations for students with disabilities* (pp. 5–10). Minneapolis: National Center on Educational Outcomes, University of Minnesota.

American Psychological Association. (1985). *Standards for educational and psychological testing.* Washington, DC: Author.

Archbald, D. A. (1991). Authentic assessment: Principles, practices, and issues. *School Psychology Quarterly, 6,* 279–293.

Archbald, D. A., & Newmann, F. (1988). *Beyond standardized testing: Assessing authentic academic achievement in the secondary school.* Reston, VA: National Association of Secondary School Principals.

Baker, E. L. (1990, October). *Assessment and public policy: Does validity matter?* Paper presented at the annual meeting of the American Evaluation Association, Washington, DC.

Baker, E. L, O'Neil, H. F., Jr., & Linn, R. L. (1993). Policy and validity prospects for performance-based assessment. *American Psychologist, 48,* 1210–1218.

Buros, O. K. (1933). *Educational, psychological, and personality tests of 1933 and 1934.* New Brunswick, NJ: Gryphon.

Cizek, G. J. (1991). Confusion effusion: A rejoinder to Wiggins. *Phi Delta Kappan, 73,* 150–153.

Coutinho, M., & Malouf, D. (1992, November). *Performance assessment and children with disabilities: Issues and possibilities.* Washington, DC: Division of Innovation and Development, U.S. Department of Education.

Cronbach, L. J. (1990). *Essentials of psychological testing* (5th ed.). New York: HarperCollins.

Deno, S. (1985). Curriculum-based measurement: The emerging alternative. *Exceptional Children, 52,* 219–232.

Dunbar, S. B., Koretz, D., & Hoover, H. D. (1991).Quality control in the development and use of performance assessments. *Applied Measurement in Education, 4,* 289–302.

Elliott, S. N. (1991). Authentic assessment: An introduction to a neobehavioral approach to classroom assessment. *School Psychology Quarterly, 6,* 273–278.

Elliott, S. N. (1993, August). *Performance assessment: Dogma, data, and technical issues.* Paper presented at the annual meeting of the American Psychological Association, Toronto, Canada.

Federal Resource Center for Special Education. (1993, May). *Task force report: Cultural and linguistic diversity in education.* Lexington: Human Development Institute, University of Kentucky.

Fuchs, L. S. (1994). *Integrating performance assessment with instructional decision making: Lessons from the past, implications for the future.* Reston, VA: The Council for Exceptional Children.

Gardner, H. (1986). *The mind's new science.* New York: Basic Books.

Gipps, C. V. (1993, April). *Reliability, validity, and manageability in large scale performance assessment.* Paper presented at the meeting of the American Educational Research Association, Atlanta, GA.

Goldman, S. R., Pellegrino, J. W., & Bransford, J. (in press). Assessing programs that invite thinking. In E. L. Baker & H. F. O'Neil, Jr. (Eds). *Technology assessment in education and training.* Hillsdale, NJ: Erlbaum.

Hawkins, J., Collins, A., & Frederiksen, J. (1990, September). *Interactive technologies and the assessment of learning.* Paper presented at the UCLA Center for Technology Assessment conference, Los Angeles.

Hayes, S. C., Nelson, R. O., & Jarrett, R. B. (1986). Evaluating the quality of behavioral assessment. In R. O. Nelson & S. C. Hayes (Eds.), *Conceptual foundations of behavioral assessment* (pp. 463–503). New York: Guilford.

Kane, M. T. (1992a, December). *Validating performance tests.* Unpublished manuscript, University of Wisconsin-Madison.

Kane, M. T. (1992b). An argument-based approach to validity. *Psychological Bulletin, 112,* 527–535.

Kazdin, A. (1974). Self-monitoring and behavior change. In M. J. Mahoney & C. E. Thoresen (Eds.), *Self-control: Power to the person* (pp. 218–246). Monterey, CA: Brooks-Cole.

Koretz, D., Lewis, E., Skewes-Cox, T., & Burnstein, L. (1992). *Omitted and not-reached items in mathematics in the 1990 National Assessment of Educational Progress.* (CSE Technical Report No. 357). Los Angeles: University of California, National Center for Research on Evaluation, Standards, and Student Testing.

Kratochwill, T. R. (1992). *What behavioral assessment has to contribute to authentic assessment.* Unpublished manuscript, University of Wisconsin-Madison.

Kratochwill, T. R., & Shapiro, E. S. (1988). Conceptual foundations of behavioral assessment in schools. In E. S. Shapiro & T. R. Kratochwill (Eds.), *Behavioral assessment in schools: Conceptual foundations and practical applications* (pp. 1–13). New York: Guilford.

Kratochwill, T. R., & Sheridan, S. M. (1990). Advances in behavioral assessment. In T. B. Gutkin & C. R. Reynolds (Eds.), *The handbook of school psychology* (pp. 328–364). New York: Wiley.

Linn, R. L. (1992, September) *Linking results of distinct assessments.* Paper prepared for the Council of Chief State School Officers, Washington, DC.

Linn, R. L. (1993). Educational assessment: Expanded expectations and challenges. *Educational Evaluation and Policy Analysis, 15,* 1–16.

Linn, R. L., Baker, E. L., & Dunbar, S. B. (1991). Complex, performance-based assessment: Expectations and validation criteria. *Educational Researcher, 20,* 15–21.

Madaus, G. F. (1985). Public policy and the testing profession: You've never had it so good? *Educational Measurement: Issues and Practice, 4,* 5–11.

Mehrens, W. A. (1992). Using performance assessment for accountability purposes. *Educational Measurement: Issues and Practice, 11,* 3–9, 20.

Merwin, J. (1993). Inclusion and accommodation: "You can tell what is important to a society by the things it chooses to measure." In J. E. Ysseldyke and M. L. Thurlow (Eds.), *Views on inclusion and testing accommodations for students with disabilities* (pp. 30–34). Minneapolis: National Center on Educational Outcomes: University of Minnesota.

Messick, S. (1988). The once and future issues of validity: Assessing the meaning and consequences of measurement. In H. Wainer & H. Braun (Eds.), *Test validity* (pp. 33–45). Hillsdale, NJ: Erlbaum.

Messick, S. (1989). *Validity.* In R. L. Linn (Ed.), *Educational measurement* (3rd ed., pp. 13–104). New York: Macmillan.

Messick, S. (1994). The interplay of evidence and consequences in the validation of performance assessments. *Educational Researcher, 23*(2), 13–23.

Mislevy, R. J. (1992). *Linking educational assessments: Concepts, issues, methods, and prospects.* Princeton, NJ: Educational Testing Service, Policy Information Center.

Poteet, J. A., Choate, J. S., & Stewart, S. S. (1993). Performance assessment and special education: Practices and prospects. *Focus on Exceptional Children, 26*(1), 24–29.

Queensland Department of Education. (1991). *Assessment of student performance 1990: Aspects of reading and writing.* Brisbane, Australia: Author.

Reschly, D. J. (1993). Consequences and incentives: Innovations for inclusion/exclusion decisions regarding students with disabilities in state and national assessment programs. In J. Ysseldyke & M. Thurlow (Eds.), *Views on inclusion and testing accommodations for students with disabilities* (pp. 35–46). Minneapolis: College of Education, University of Minnesota.

Resnick, L. B., & Resnick, D. P. (1992). Assessing the thinking curriculum: New tools for educational reform. In B. R. Gifford & M. C. O'Connor (Eds.), *Changing assessments: Alternative views of aptitude, achievement, and instruction* (pp. 37–75). Boston: Kluwer.

Reynolds, M. C. (1993). Inclusion and accommodation in assessment at the margins. In J. E. Ysseldyke & M. B. Thurlow (Eds.), *Views on inclusion and testing accommodations for students with disabilities* (pp. 47–63). Minneapolis: National Center on Educational Outcomes: University of Minnesota.

Shavelson, R. J., & Baxter, G. P. (1992). What we've learned about assessing hands-on science. *Educational Leadership, 49,* 20–25.

Shavelson, R. J., Baxter, G. P., & Pine, J. (1992). Performance assessments: Political rhetoric and measurement reality. *Educational Researcher, 21,* 22–27.

Shavelson, R. J., Baxter, G. P., Pine, J., Yure, J. Goldman, S. R., & Smith, B. (1991). Alternative technologies for large scale science assessment: Instrument of educational reform. *School Effectiveness and School Improvement, 2,* 97–14.

Shinn, M. R. (Ed.) (1989). *Curriculum-based measurement: Assessing special children.* New York: Guilford.

Stiggins, R. J. (1991). Facing the challenges of a new era of educational assessment. *Applied Measurement in Education, 4,* 263–274.

U.S. Congress, Office of Technology Assessment. (1992, February). *Testing in American schools: Asking the right questions.*(OTA-SET-519). Washington, DC: U.S. Government Printing Office.

Webb, N. L. (1993, October). *Wisconsin Performance Assessment Development Project: Annual report for 1992–93.* Madison: Wisconsin Center for Educational Research, University of Wisconsin-Madison.

Wiggins, G. P. (1993). *Assessing student performance: Exploring the purpose and limits of testing.* San Francisco: Jossey-Bass.

Witte, S. P., & Vander Ark, C. (1992, September). *WSAS communication/language arts performance assessment: The Wausau workshop.* Paper prepared for the WSAS Performance Assessment Project, University of Wisconsin-Madison.

Wolf, D. P., LeMahieu, P. G., & Eresh, J. (1992). Good measure: Assessment as a tool for educational reform. *Educational Leadership, 49,* 8–13.

Ysseldyke, J. E., & Thurlow, M. L. (Eds.). (1993a). *Views on inclusion and testing accommodations for students with disabilities.* (Synthesis Report 7). Minneapolis: College of Education, University of Minnesota.

Ysseldyke, J. E., & Thurlow, M. L. (Eds.). (1993b). *Self-study guide to development of educational outcomes and indicators.* Minneapolis: College of Education, University of Minnesota.